THE
BOOK OF
TESTIMONY

Taking Roads Less Traveled

Jack M Schooley

REVISED EDITION

To contact Jack,

email: friends@creativestirrings.org

ISBN: 979-8-9864334-0-0

Wandering Stream
Literary and Publishing

jimpowell@wanderingstream.org

Acknowledgements

To all my loved ones who have walked with
me over the last forty-plus years:
There is no way to thank you enough!

A special thanks to Jim Powell and
his lovely wife, Ann; whose encouragement
kept me on my quest to serve my King.

TABLE OF CONTENTS

FOREWARD

Pioneers and settlers — two people types necessary to take new territory in older times. Pioneers took on difficult assignments, like of sailing unnavigated seas, cutting raw trails and finding suitable lands for creating change. Settlers followed and transformed these new places, making them habitable.

Life comes together differently for settlers and pioneers, though. Settlers prefer a life of familiarity, repetition and safety with the challenges of the unknown left to the pioneers. Forerunning pioneers take risks without assurances and move life forward without a plan B — resourcefully winging it with invisible wisdom. That's the pioneer life.

Jack is a pioneer. Inventive, creative and resourceful, he intuitively took up the trail clues of the road less traveled, and navigated them with God as his companion. He created change while nobody watched, designed helpful inventions and improved the well-being of those around him.

This testimony is a memoir of a life taking roads less traveled without signposts or GPS — just a still small voice to guide. He knew something most of us know but don't believe.

Yahweh is with us wherever we go. It's a promise stated multiple times in scripture. For those with the courage to believe it, it's a reflection of what God can do with ordinary people for extraordinary purposes; courageous people like Jack, you and I.

These excerpts of Jack's life are meant to stir you. And we all need creative stirrings to move us into the unknown byways of the Kingdom of God. There we experience the glorious life of dependence on the Lord.

And after all is done, Jack can claim, as Robert Frost did in his famous poem: "And that has made all the difference." Allow his words to inspire you to give yourself permission and gain courage to explore the roads of spiritual unknowns. It *will* make all the difference.

Jim Powell

Long-time friend of Jack

Preface

Why this book about my personal testimony?

I want to tell everyone I can of all the good things I got to do with God before I leave here. This book gives me opportunity to continue to share these events after I'm gone. It is my desire to reveal his goodness.

At the time of writing this preface, I had been trying to do what my Father in heaven had asked me to do for upwards of 45 years. And I'm still doing that. This is not to say I had done it well. I'm sure I did more than what He asked me to do on occasion.

Most times it was through hindsight that I could look back and see His leading and handy work. Other times, I fully knew what He wanted me to do. His verbal marching orders were often hard for me to do without grumbling, or having a bad attitude. Thankfully, He was always understanding and patient with me.

And I never felt or believed He was anything other than kind and loving. That's grace.

I don't claim to be a prophet, although I feel I have stood in the sandals of one. I've been told to do what I thought was some crazy stuff. And I can only assume that I was the best choice for those illogical jobs.

This collection of testimonies are highlights of my walk with Jesus. I have not listed them in any strict order of time and date. For example, the first testimony is about my trip to India in 2014. The reason was to prepare this book for translation into the Tamil language.

Each testimony stands on its own merit to point to the One who gave them life.

A Little Testimony to Start

I was seated on the podium getting ready to preach at a two-day pastor's conference in Coimbatore, India. God's presence was strong and tears rained down my face. The Lord said to me, "I have given you India."

I snapped back at Him out loud, "I don't want it. I already have China and I don't know what to do with it." I leaned over at Bill. He was one of the other speakers. I told him what the Lord had said. He smiled and told me he heard what the Lord was saying, and I was to speak first. I was to speak to about a hundred pastors and I realized I had nothing to say.

The tears kept coming, even after I got up and stood at the microphone. I was crying and I was embarrassed; a grown man, standing there crying. Nothing was coming to my mind. I was brain dead.

I looked towards the music equipment next to the keyboard, and there stood a special microphone holder that I had invented twenty years before. When I first got up to preach the interpreter from had come up and stood next to me. I looked at him and pointed to the mic-holder and said, "I invented that twenty years ago and sold it all over America."

The interpreter's expression went from black to white. He staggered back a step and looked shocked. With a shaky voice and tears streaming down his face he said, "One year ago, I had a dream that a man came to speak at a church and he pointed to that microphone holder and said, 'I invented that twenty years ago and sold it all over America.' Then I awoke from my dream. I did not understand the meaning of the dream until now.' He had only seen the mic-holder before in that dream.

I put my hand on his chest. And as we sobbed together, I proclaimed him a true prophet of God to India. This alone was worth the trip.

How I Got to India

I was asked to go on that trip to India by a good friend. He and I traveled together across China the year before. I told him I had been to India before and had not lost anything there. So I said to him, "No thanks, and have a great trip."

To start with I didn't want to spend the money. A few weeks later he called back and asked me to reconsider. I gave him the same answer and then he said he would pay for my trip. I again said no and added, "I don't like India."

I hung up the phone feeling relieved that I didn't have to go; it's a long trip. Besides, he wanted to be gone over Thanksgiving. My wife said to me, "I think you should go. He needs your help. Just be back by Thanksgiving."

Reluctantly, I got back to him and said I would go. He wanted to go for a month. I could only go for two weeks; returning Thanksgiving eve. He was fine with it.

My attitude about India changed during that conference. The miracle of the microphone holder had a great impact on my heart.

Checking my travel plan home on Thanksgiving eve, one stop arrived at 3:30 pm at JFK airport. Not fun, it would be packed. I tried to change my ticket with no luck. I flew from Coimbatore to Mumbai, with an eight-hour layover. I spent four hours in the Mumbai Starbucks sharing some of my testimonies and leading a young Swiss couple to the Lord. I also prayed with them for healing. When I got to JFK, the airport looked deserted; hardly a soul in sight. Remember, this is Thanksgiving eve. I spent three more hours sharing with a young Asian girl, and then flew home to Portland arriving at 9:30 pm, a half hour early.

Here is the miracle. On every flight I had an empty seat next to me. I arrived rested and thankful. And happy to have a great turkey dinner.

A Little Personal History

About six months after getting saved and then leading my mother and stepfather to the Lord, my mother told me this story; it was 1970. As I mulled over the story, I guessed it must have happened in December of 1943.

First you must understand that my mother was a very beautiful woman. And in her day, she was a stage performer and model in San Francisco. Pictures and newspaper articles showed her dining with west coast mafia bosses. All those pictures were destroyed in a flood on our ranch in northern Washington around 1971.

Several elements about my mother's life are unusual. I was around twelve years old and living with my grandmother. She told me some stories. Of which, t wo really stand out.

When my mother was a little girl about four years old, she sang and danced for San Francisco children's talent contests.

One afternoon a big car pulled into the yard at the family homestead. A man got out of the car and knocked on the door. He was invited in for a drink. The man claimed to be some kind of movie producer and promoter from Hollywood. He offered a contract to my grandmother for my mother to sing and dance on stage and in the movies. My grandfather absolutely refused to sign and said that no daughter of his would be that kind of lowlife stage performer; or something to that effect. My grandmother said, "Your mother could have been like Shirley Temple."

Later, when my mother was in her late teens she modeled in San Francisco and performed on stages all around Northern California. She got herself hooked up with some mafia bosses in San Francisco. They signed her to a contract to make movies in Hollywood. Taking her to Hollywood on the train, they locked her in a cheap third floor hotel room. Instead of making movies she was kidnapped to be put in the white-slave trade.

My mother told me the rest of the story later. After three days of being locked in the hotel with no food, she broke out the bathroom window and climbed down the sewer pipe attached to the outside wall of the brick hotel. She made her way to a Western Union office and wired home for money so she could take the bus back to Napa.

Afterward, she met and married my father. This is the part of the story that made me sit up and wonder. In December of 1943 my father and mother were walking through a carnival that was set up between Napa and Vallejo, California; Vallejo being my birthplace.

My mother told me they were walking arm in arm past one of the tents and a lady came out. She walked up to my mother and put her finger on her flat stomach and said, "The man child you carry in your womb will serve the living God." And then the woman turned and walked away. My mother told me with a very serious look on her face, "I did not know I was pregnant." I was born the following July in 1944.

We lived in Vallejo for some years. My first memory is that of my sister being baptized at a church across the street from where I attended kindergarten.

My father left for the Korean war. Once he was gone, we never lived together as a family from that time on. I remember more of my Fathers brother, Uncle Bob. Uncle Bob was on the police force in Vallejo; a ruff Navy town. And my father was the local tuff guy.

Dad had become a professional boxer sometime before the war and he practiced on everyone in town including my sister and me. I was told this by my Aunt Marie and Uncle Bob. Uncle Bob would find my sister and I walking lower Georgia Street; the worst part of Vallejo. We would be going in and out of the bars looking for my mother. Sometimes at 2 or 3 in the morning. He would scoop us up, put us in his cruiser and take us to his house where my Aunt would change my diapers, feed us, put us down to sleep. And then my Uncle Bob would go out and find my mother.

On the Redwood Road
Healing at Nine Years Old

My mother met a man while working at Mare Island Naval Ship Yard. They married and we moved to Napa, California to live in his large ranch house on Redwood road. Across the road and running through his property was Redwood Creek. I spent a lot of time trout fishing along this beautiful stream. As I walked along the stream, I would keep the lead shot tucked in my cheek. So, when I needed a little more weight on the fishing line, the shots were readily available. I managed to swallow several of them.

Remember, this was around 1953 and few people had any idea what lead would do to the body. The next school year, I missed a lot of school. I was always tired and my legs and joints ached most of the time. The doctor said I had rheumatic fever. They held me back a whole year because of the illness.

I was very sick one day. My grandmother got me up and took me to see a lady in Napa. Her name was Nola and she was a Christian

Scientist practitioner. Nola was an old, white haired grandma, just like my grandmother. It seemed like she knew what she was doing. My grandmother said, "just listen to her and try to believe what she says." It felt natural to do that at the time. She said, "You cannot be sick; you are made in the image and likeness of God." I trusted her and believed what she said.

The next day I just could not lay on the couch any longer, watching that black and white television. I headed outside and found my wagon. I was healed.

The next Sunday night, my mom and grandma took me to a church in Napa. I saw Nola the Practitioner there. I stood up in the service and gave my first testimony of how God had healed me.

Schoolwork was much harder after that; I could not concentrate on learning. So, I just started reading books and never stopped.

Finding My Way to the Pacific Northwest

I spent my high school years in Mountain View, California. I also worked on cars and went on great adventures with my school chums.

School was very boring. But the trouble was, I could not remember what I read or what I was taught. I struggled through each day — chewing lead sinkers while fishing had taken its toll.

At the beginning of tenth grade, I told my mother I just could not do school anymore. I wanted to work in a machine shop that my current girl friend's father managed. She agreed, and I worked there for a year. Afterward, I moved back to Vallejo and lived with my sister and her husband.

I applied at Mare Island Naval Ship Yard in Vallejo and got hired as a helper in Shop 31, a nuclear division machine shop. I helped run some of the machines and built all sorts of cool stuff for my 4-wheel drive rig.

After that first year it was time for my vacation. I went to see my father, who lived in Seattle and worked for Boeing Aircraft. My father and I spent a little time getting reacquainted. Then he suggested I go to Boeing and apply for a machinist job. He said anybody could get a job there. They had just gotten a big contract for the new 747 that was being developed.

I went and filled out an application, exaggerating my qualifications. They hired me as an experimental machinist and gave me a two thousand dollar signing bonus. When I got home to Vallejo, a moving truck was parked in front of my house ready to move all my possessions to a nice house in Seattle Boeing had rented for me. That was really cool.

I was now a bonafide machinist — I could do this. I loaded the rest of my stuff and headed north to Seattle and the great adventure. When I got there, I took some of the signing bonus and stopped at a machine shop tool store. I just walked in and asked for a toolbox with whatever tools were needed to become a machinist. The guy behind the counter gave me a funny look and

I just shrugged my shoulders. I confessed that I didn't know what tools they would expect me to have.

I carried my new toolbox to the basement of the wind tunnel at Boeing's Development Center. It was the very best as far as machine shops were concerned. And of course, they hired the best machinists. This was a great and happy moment. I had made it to the big time without even going through the four-year apprenticeship.

The supervisor's name was Russ. He showed me the lay out of the shop and directed me to put my tool box on the bench next to a sweet looking little lathe. I had seen one like it before at Mare Island in Shop 31. He gave my brand-new metal toolbox a real long look. I followed him to a desk where he introduced me to the leading man and handed me a drawing.

The he gave me a chunk of steel and said, "This piece of steel cost us $30,000 [1960s dollars]. Now don't screw it up." I said, "No problem" and walked back to my machine.

I opened the drawing and after sometime got it turned up the right way. It said in a little box down in the right-hand corner that it was a wind tunnel sting. I thought, *How do they expect me to make this if I have never seen one before.*

I looked back and forth between the drawing and the machine, then walked over to a guy running a machine like the one I had in front me and introduced myself. We exchanged a little small talk, then I asked him if he would show me how to turn on my lathe. He thought I was joking with him, but proceeded to walk over and push the button for me. Great, now I was in business.

Without him knowing it, I watched him use his machine. I walked to the tool room to get a tool that would do what he was doing. When I asked the tool guy for a tool, he gave me this blank stare. "Sonny," he answered gruffly, "we make our own tools here." Then he turned and walked away.

Great, I thought, *I will just have to go find one to copy.* And I did.

After six months on the job, I advanced to grade 2. Grade 1 was the top of the food chain.

SAVED BY BACK SURGERY

A few years into working at Boeing, I decided to take a trip to Europe for my first vacation. I did my homework and got a schedule laid out. I would fly to Rome and spend a few days. Then off to Germany and France before heading home. A sweet little trip. I bought my luggage and some new clothes — I was ready to go!

One day at work, a week before my flight was scheduled to depart, I started having horrible pains down my legs. They took my breath away. I left work and found a doctor. They took x-rays then told me I needed surgery — fast.

I said, "How about after the trip?"

They responded, "You're not going on a trip."

After surgery, I was resting at home on the couch in my body cast and watching TV. A news special came on stating, "We have just received word that flight 000 From Rome, Italy to Frankfurt, Germany has gone down in the Mediterranean Sea with no survivors."

That was my flight.

Becoming a Mountain Man

After four years at Boeing, the company had a big layoff. It was 1969. I moved to Leavenworth, Washington; on the east side of the Cascades. I spent the summer working on a pack string as a guide and clearing the Pacific Crest Trail. I did not like the job much so, I decided I would immigrate to Canada and start a homestead.

The land was out of Hudson Hope, north of Prince George, British Columbia. There was a new dam on the river and the lake it created opened up unexplored territory. I bought all my stuff for the adventure. I got a canoe, boots, winter coat; you name it I had it.

I sent my application to the Canadian government and was promptly rejected due to the Vietnam War. They didn't want more draft dodgers in their country. I felt unfairly treated. I was no draft dodger. I was classified 1Y, which meant I had a deferment because of a bad back.

I called my mother and Bill and told them I was going to buy a 70-acre ranch in the Methow Valley of northern Washington. They threw in with me and moved to the ranch. They stayed the first winter then headed back to California to live the good life.

SALVATION

In the winter of 1970, I had taken a job working graveyard shift as a machinist for a sawmill in Omak, Washington. A young millwright named Jim Reid came by the lathe I was running. He looked me in the eye and said, "Do you know Jesus?" My response was, "Yes, I know about him." He turned and walked away.

From the time my sister got baptized, I believed that there was a God and that He made everything back there in Genesis. I followed the beliefs of Herbert W. Armstrong's "Worldwide Church of God" for some years when my mother and stepfather had sought God's approval. I had not given it serious thought, so it wasn't making a difference in my life.

The next night Jim stopped by my lathe again. We chatted and began a relationship that I needed at the time. For the preceding year, my do Moochie and I had lived alone in a cabin on 70 acres back up against the Okanogan National Forest along the Methow Valley of North Central Washington. It was 70 miles from the saw mill.

Jim stopped by the machine shop one night to tell me what he was doing at his church and ask me if I would come and help. On Wednesday night he took care of the young children that were three to five years old.

I said, "That would be great! I have nothing to do"!

The next night was Wednesday, so I drove into Omak early for church and helped him take care of the kids. I had a great time meeting people and enjoying the little sweethearts.

After the service, Jim took me to the local Christian coffee house in Okanogan. After coffee we went to the sawmill to work. The next week, Jim came by the machine shop and asked me if I would come to dinner at his home the next night. I was thrilled. I had been very troubled about my life and the emptiness I felt since meeting him.

Around 7 PM, I arrived at Jim's home in Mallott, Washington;

just south of Okanogan. Jim introduced me to his family, then informed me that the sawmill supervisor had called. The equipment had broken down and he was needed at work. He told me to stay and help his wife cook dinner, bathe his four boys and put them to bed. Then I was to come to work at my regular time.

I look back over that evening and wonder what Jim's lovely young wife was thinking and feeling. At that time, I was a young powerful man with long wavy hair and a full black beard. I was dressed in a plaid shirt, dirty Levi's. I had a knife and a 357 magnum on my belt and people called me Coon Skin Schooley.

After we cooked and ate dinner, I bathed the boys while she cleaned the kitchen and put the dishes away. When we had finished, we sat down at the kitchen table. She looked at me and said, "Would you like to go through the plan of salvation with me?" I said, "Sure! That would be fine." She pulled out a flip chart and laid a Bible on the table in front of me. She read through the chart with me while I looked up and read scriptures. When we finished reading the chart and looking up scriptures, we turned to the last page. On it was a picture of Jesus and a prayer of commitment. It took me forty-five minutes and a box of tissue to get through that prayer. I was miraculously converted.

I had to tell someone. I ran from the house, jumped in my car and headed for the Christian coffee house in Okanogan. Inside were a lot of people waiting for me. They were jumping up and down and having a party. They had been praying for me. Jim's wife had called ahead and told them what had happened.

Bethesda

I read the Word through spring and tried a few local churches. But I wasn't satisfied with what I was experiencing. an orchardist in Pateros, Washington told me about a move of the Holy Spirit that was happening in Wenatchee, about an hour drive south of the ranch. I headed down to Wenatchee and found the church exciting and lively. So I started making the 140-mile round trip drive twice a week.

Not long after on a Wednesday night, the pastor's mother; the late Rachel Titus; came to me and asked if I had received the baptism of the Holy Spirit. I told her I had read about it, but did not know how to do it. She took me into one of the classrooms and began to pray for me. I closed my eyes and felt her gently touch my head. Tears began to stream down my face and I raised my hands and began to sing in a beautiful voice a song in a language I had never heard before. After singing for some time, I began to sing the same song in English. This was wonderful and I don't remember how long I worshiped. When I finally opened my eyes, Rachel was gone, the church was locked and I was the only one left inside.

I made my way to my car and began the 70-mile drive home. When I pulled onto the road that followed the Columbia River north from Wenatchee, the song in the spirit returned along with the interpretation and tears running down my cheeks. Going around a sharp bend in the road, I got on the wrong side. I managed to just miss a police car and get back on my side.

At the next turnout I pulled over and waited. It wasn't long and blue flashing lights pulled in behind me. Still singing my song, crying and looking out the rearview mirror, I watched him get out of his curser. He adjusted his holster and cap. I got out and walked toward him. I took out my wallet and pulled my driver's license.

Offering my license, I said, "I have had such a wonderful experience. I would like to tell you about it." He took a hard look at the license and began backing away as I shared the joy of receiving the Holy Spirit. He backpedaled faster as I bore down on him. Jamming my license back in my hand, he turned and jumped into his curser then yelled, "Slow down!" He spun his car around in the dirt and sped away.

I arrived home to find my cabin filled with other new believers. I shared my experience and they too wanted the filling of the Holy Spirit.

Trusting the Lord

I left my job at the sawmill believing I had a higher calling. By September, I found myself sitting in my cabin with no food and $13 to my name. While I prayed and read the Word, I stumbled on the scripture that says He will provide all my needs according to His riches in glory. I bowed my head and asked, "Lord I need food."

At that moment I sensed in my Spirit, "Go get you hunting license." I struggled with this because a hunting license at that time was $12. That would leave me with $1. I finally gave in, drove to Pateros and went to the liquor store to buy my license; the only place to get one. I walked to the counter and declared, "God told me to get my hunting license." The lady shook her head with a strange smirk on her face. She pulled out the licensing book and started to write.

When she was done, I gave her the money then headed to see

the pastor of the Church of Christ. I told him my story. He laughed and said, "Well, let's go hunting."

I said, "Well, I would take you but I can't hunt because I don't need to. God will bring the deer to me because it said in the scripture that He will provide." I received a stern lecture on the responsibility to do my part, then we went hunting. I sat in the truck and waited four hours for him to come back. He was empty handed. On the ride home I received another lecture. I dropped him off at his place and headed home.

The next morning, I woke with a start and looked at my clock. It said 6 AM. I felt an urge to look out the window next to my bed. Standing at the barbed wire fence on my property line about 40 yards away was the most beautiful 4-point buck I had ever seen. He was looking at me looking at him from my window. I jumped out of bed, pulled on my Levi's, grabbed my 7 mm magnum and ran for the door. When I stepped outside the buck had turned and was walking slowly up the steep hill along the fence. I pulled down on him and fired. The buck just kept slowly walking. I threw another round in the chamber and fired again. I saw the bullet hit the dirt 20 yards from the deer. I slumped down realizing my scope was off. I just could not believe I missed at 50 yards with

10-power scope. but the buck was gone.

I went back in the cabin, sat down at my kitchen table and put my head in my hands. My dog Moochie sat across from me not saying a word. After just a few minutes I heard this still small voice say to me, "Take your knife and climb the hill." I took my knife and followed after the buck. A few steps from where I first shot, I rounded a large sage bush. The buck was laying there with his head downhill. At closer look, I saw where the bullet had cut through the skin of his neck, severing the artery. Provision from the Lord had been provided according to his Word.

I hung the deer in my shed and went back in the cabin. When I sat down the phone rang. The owner of the little store in the berg of Methow asked if I would come and work for him cutting meat. If I did, he would pay me with groceries from his store. I packed my gift from God into my pickup truck and headed for work.

Healing & The Calling

Six months after receiving the baptism of the Holy Spirit, I was led to attend the World Map conference that was annually held on the Washington coast. The keynote speaker that year was Charles Tromley from Texas. After an afternoon meeting, he conducted a healing service. His focus at that service pointed to people with legs that were not of equal length. He would have the people sit in a chair than hold up their legs to reveal the difference. When he prayed, legs grew equal length and the person's back problem would be corrected.

As I observed people getting healed, the thought came to me that if their healing were really a gift of the Holly Spirit, it would not matter who spoke the words or if the words were even heard. The next lady to sit in the chair had a very short leg. Charles lifted her legs and everyone gasped. At that moment I whispered, "Grow in the name of Jesus." Charles said, "Why look at that. I did not even have time to pray and the leg has grown out."

A chill ran through me. Then I turned and left the building. I walked to a beautiful grassy area and fell on my knees under a large oak tree. I was stunned at what had happened. I began to just whisper the name of Jesus. After a few seconds I began to speak these words, "Before I formed you in the womb, I knew you. Before you were born, I set you apart. I appointed you as a prophet to the nations. Lord, I do not know how to speak; I am only a child. Do not say you are a child. You must go to everyone I send you and say whatever I command you. Do not be afraid of them for I am with you." It was from Jeremiah 1: 4-8.

This Word burned in me. I didn't know what to do with it. After recovering my wits, I made my way to Charles Trombley's cabin. I knocked and he asked me to come in. I described what had happened and he opened the Word to Jeremiah chapter 1 and asked me if I had ever read it. I told him I did not know about that book in the bible. I asked Charles what it meant and he said, "Looks like you are called to be a prophet to the nations." I had no idea what that meant.

First Prophetic Act

A few days later I was led to a group of cabins tucked back in the Cascades west of Twisp, Washington. I drove up a dirt road that opened into a large clearing with ten cabins around the edge. I parked my car and climbed the steps to the first cabin. I knocked and waited for the door to open. A young man opened and stood looking at me. I looked past him and saw three other men on their knees in the kitchen.

The man said, "Can I help you"?

I told him, "The Lord sent me."

He praised the Lord and asked me to join the fellowship in the kitchen. I sat at the kitchen table and said, "You have a bad seed amongst you and you must ask it to leave". At that, they began to thank the Lord, then became sad and wept. The four men had been praying, asking the Lord what to do about one of the couples living in one of the cabins. They had been making trouble for the rest of the families.

Moving to Wenatchee

The Church in Wenatchee was the place to be. The move of the Spirit was wonderful and the pastor was Larry Titus. His mother was Prophetess Rachel Titus who prayed with me to receive the Holy Spirit. Bethesda Christian Center was filled with musically gifted people and so many pastors were discipled and trained by Larry Titus.

A few months before, while living up Squaw Creek in Methow Valley, I met and married a wonderful young woman that taught school in Brewster, Washington. Not too long after that we moved to Wenatchee to be part of what the Lord was doing.

I got hired as a salesman at the local Radio Shack. The owner was pleased with my sales ability. God blessed me and after the first month I was top salesman in the Pacific Northwest district.

During a lull in business one afternoon, I wandered back to

the office area. The boss's office was at the top of some steps so he could look out a one-way window to keep an eye out for shoplifters. I took the two steps up to the landing, then stopped and leaned against the handrail. Jerry the owner, was seated at his desk. He leaned back in his chair and welcomed me in to have a chat. Just as he leaned back in his office chair, I heard this small voice say, "Speak to him."

What came out of my mouth was a language I had never heard. Jerry grabbed a pen and started tapping it on the desk for all he was worth. Jerry said to me, "Is that what they call speaking in tongues?" I answered, "Yes."

Jerry responded, "Well, that is not so bad." I stood there looking at him for a time waiting. Then Jerry said, "You know I am a Baptist. We don't do that. But I would like you to come over to the house and show my wife how you do that".

I said, "Ok!"

I was invited to their home on a Saturday. It was a nice hot central Washington summer afternoon. When I arrived, there were about fifteen people sitting around the pool, waiting for the BBQ to do its work. After eating and a little chit chat, Jerry called us into his front room and directed us to sit on the floor in a big circle. This was the 70's and we were all practicing the love and bumper sticker lifestyle.

Jerry told everyone to take hands and let them know I was going to pray. Everyone bowed their head and it was quiet. I opened my mouth and began to speak in a strange but not unfamiliar language. It was a short burst. When I stopped the guy sitting next to me said loudly, "I know what you said. That is Portuguese, my second language. You said, "I am the living God, come to me and you will be saved."

I thought it was nice. I was still very young in the Lord and very impressed. After the interpretation of the message in tongues, some began to cry. I asked if they would like to be baptized out in the pool. Several were baptized. Jerry and his wife, Amy, were first in line.

Being Part of the Church

I jumped into ministry, starting a new outreach into Poland and Czechoslovakia; now known as the Czech Republic. I made cassette tapes of some of the best teaching of the seventies. We smuggled them in to the country with the help of the underground church. I also had a half hour radio program called, "Teachings in The Word by Christian Audio."

It was the custom at that time, to dress in suit and tie for every service. I tried to conform to that standard as best I could. And I always sat in the front row with Rachel Titus and Kay Pugh; I had become their escort. I would take them to lunch and dinner after service and sometimes during the week.

One Sunday morning while seated in the front row next to the spiritual queen bees (That was what we thought of them. We just loved them and they were a major part of the churches discipleship program), I began thinking. *What was it like to sit up in the balcony overlooking the service?* The urge to sit next to the sound system up there became very strong. I excused myself while the service was well under way and made my it up the stairs and sat next to the soundman. From there I could see across the whole stage. It was beautiful.

Have you ever seen one of those Disney Cartoons where the colors begin to rain from the top of the screen and down across the picture changing the scene? That is exactly what saw. It rained the most beautiful colors across the front of that service. What appeared to me was the face of Jesus. It made me gasp.

Out of the corner of my eye I saw the soundman give me a look. After a few minutes of ecstasy, I could not contain the joy I felt. I jumped to my feet and ran down the stairs to the microphone on the stage. Larry very graciously stepped back and let me share the vision with the church. At times now, when I am praying, I see colors changing and the face of Jesus is there.

We were living in a one-bedroom apartment in Wenatchee. It was common to have college kids live with us. After six months in the apartment, I asked the Lord for a bigger place. A few days later I heard his still small voice say, "Get up and go outside." I did so and I found the land Lord digging around the front of the apartment. I asked him boldly, "Do you have a house you can sell me?" He blinked a few times and responded, "Fsunny you would ask this. My mother passed away about a month ago and I did not know what I would do with her house. It is a five-bedroom old home that needs some fixing up. Would you like to take a look at it?" I told him I would.

I met him at the home a few days later and the place was just what I wanted. He took me to the bank and we wrote up a six-month lease with option to buy. We rented out two of the rooms to college kids and they helped me fix the place up. At the end of six months, I still had no money for the down payment. When I told the owner of the property I had not been able to save the down payment, he drove me to his bank. We wrote up a new contract using my investment in repairing the home as the down payment. The house was mine.

Everything was going well for me until the business director of the church asked for all the money from my business account as a donation. Well, I got offended and gave him the whole business, sold our home that the Lord had given me and moved to Spokane to take over a Radio Shack store.

That lasted two years. My wife and I had a son and daughter and I began to treat my hyperactive son the same way my father treated me. One day I came home and my wife was gone with the children. I have not seen them since. In those days, we did not have the counseling or any drugs that could help with my son's, and my own, ADHD problems.

I packed what I had and moved back to Wenatchee. I knew I had an anger problem and needed to get back to Doctor Jesus for a cure.

Radio Shack put me to work in the north Wenatchee shopping mall where I had started with Jerry. I moved into a house with two single guys named Joe. One Joe weighed three hundred pounds and the other weighed one hundred. I was in the middle at two hundred pounds. We were quite a threesome.

Once, they wanted me to meet a friend of theirs that attended our church. We hopped in the car, drove to Sambo's Restaurant, sat in a booth and waited for service. A young lady approached to take our order. She wore a babushka and an oversized dress covered in maple syrup. I thought she was the sweetest thing I had ever seen. They introduced me to her. We ate, jumped back in the car and headed home. On our way I told to the two Joes, "I think that is my next wife." They laughed and stated that she was too good for me.

The next day was Sunday. So I prepared my best suit and washed up my silver Cadillac Eldorado. I met the two Joes at the church. I stuck one Joe at one exit and the other at the other exit. I paced between the two looking for this sweet girl from Sambo's. As I walked past the lady's bathroom the door swung open and almost knocked me down. There she was in a beautiful red dress. Her looks almost knocked me down a second time.

I took Darlene out for lunch that day. And for the next six months we enjoyed many great times together. We also sang in the choir and served in a variety of places. Unfortunately, the church began to show problems, and in time fell apart.

I got a job offer with a friend in Bend, Oregon. But after moving, I began to Miss Darlene and decided I would like to marry her. I gave Darlene a call from Bend and asked for her hand in marriage over the phone. She agreed to be my wife.

The friends that I worked for in Bend took us to Coeur d'Alene, Idaho. Pastor John Sandford married us in their home. Afterward, Darlene and I moved to California and took jobs. I went to work at FMC Corporation in San Jose and she went to work at the phone company.

Around the World

After 9 months living in Fremont, California, I felt impressed to quit our jobs and take a trip around the world. I was convinced it was the thing to do and Darlene agreed we should go. Our purpose was to see what God was doing around the world and find our place in ministry.

We put our stuff in storage and headed for Washington, stopping off in Salem, Oregon to see Larry Turner. He was Darlene's music pastor that she had served with in Grants Pass. He had since then moved to Westgate Assembly in West Salem.

Larry and his wife, Martha, did not hold back on the hospitality; inviting us to stay in their home. We shared our desires to travel around the world with Larry. He suggested that we visit the YWAM base in Salem. Graham Kerr, the famous chef, was director at the base in Salem. Graham was very helpful and suggested we visit the YWAM bases around the world. He gave us a list and we wrote them to say we were coming.

Darlene and I traveled to Yakima, Washington to visit Rachel Titus and Kay Pugh, Rachel's traveling companion. We spent a few days with them and attended a service at their home church, Shiloh Temple. The pastor was wonderful and we had dinner with him and his family of believers.

Rachel and Kay mentioned that we could get a real good deal with United Airlines. We called and discovered they had a special ticket for $1,200 each called, "Around the World in 80 Days." We could get off and on the plane as many times as we like as long as we kept going the same direction. We headed east.

First, we visited the bases in England. Then, we stayed three days at the Hurlock Castle base in Germany. We met some lady's there who asked us to drive them in their van across Germany and through Vienna to a Castle in Piobock Austria. Of course, we decided to help them.

We then flew from Munich Germany to Israel for a week. We walked where Jesus walked and toured His birthplace in Bethlehem and flew to Frankfurt. After spending two days in the airport, it was time to go.

In New Deli, India, the trip gets interesting. We arrived at the international airport at 4:30 AM. They loaded us onto a bus at the plane to take us to the immigration sight and we came very close to having our bus collide with another bus on the tarmac. The darkness of the waiting area was lit by one 100-watt light bulb with only 25 watts running through it. All we could just see was the whites of the eyes of staff people. They squatted in corners with their airport records piled from floor to the ceiling around the room; very cozy.

While on our flight from Frankfurt to New Deli we met a young couple flying from England. They were returning to their birth place to visit family. They had a beautiful little baby with them that we helped take care of on the plane. We struck up a friendship with them and they invited us to stay at their family's home overlooking the Taj Mahal. We accepted.

The young couple went through customs ahead of us and met up with waiting family members. We heard them talking back and forth and saw them pointing at us. The volume of their dialog grew louder. Then the young man we befriended came back and said, "My family could not have Christians come and be in their home, sorry." He turned and they were gone, leaving Darlene and I looking at each other and not believing our ears.

We had set our hearts on visiting Indian people in their homes and enjoying some travel with them. The young couple had said on the plane we would not need much money and that we could stay in their home as long as we were in India. A small problem had just grown into a big one. You see, when we left the USA we made arrangements to have money wired to us in Germany. It never happened.

We spent our travel money in Israel, believing that $1,000 would be waiting for us when we returned. Now, we were in the new Deli Airport at 4:30 in the morning without enough money to stay. We had made arrangements with the YWAM base in New Deli, but did not know a worldwide faith conference was being hosted by the government of India which affected accommodations at the base. We woke them up when we called to inform them we were waiting at the airport for a ride. They let us know there was not a room for us. They added that if we took the bus to get there, there was room on the floor.

We went to the bus stop and bought a ticket, but couldn't get our stuff on the bus. Once again, we stood there looking at each other. Exhausted from travel and jet lag and our patience was at an end. Darlene's eyes kept saying, "Do something." I just couldn't think of anything to do.

Desperate for sleep, we found a 1-star hotel across from the airport that had a room. We found a porter that knew of the hotel and started to walk there. It wasn't far, but a herd of burrows ran through the cars and nearly knocking us over. Our 1-star hotel was a dark and dreary sight. We quickly realized 1-star does not mean the same thing worldwide.

It was now six in the morning and we were waking up the whole place. The lady behind the counter said they had a room. But it would take some time to get the person staying there out of it. We sat down to wait.

About 8 AM we heard a screaming commotion coming from a room just around the corner. Shortly after, four guys carried a screaming man past us and deposited him outside with the pig that lived in the ditch at front of the hotel. They said he was demon possessed. They also said we could now have our room. It would cost $25 — half of our travel money.

We grabbed our bags and headed for our room. Finally, we could get some rest. The room had a double bed covered in brown sheets, one brown blanket and a brown bedspread. No doubt all these had been white at one time. We set our bags down, returned to the desk and asked for clean towels, linens and blankets. The lady behind the desk smiled and said that was all they had.

By this time, we were tired to the point of collapse. Going back to the room, we sat down on the bed and tried to think of a way to escape the nightmare. We were broke, and in a strange country with no way to get help, money or sleep. We couldn't think straight and wanted sleep more than anything. So, we decided to simply hunker down.

We went back to the desk and asked for pillowcases. In a few minutes we had brown pillowcases from the room next to ours. Improvising, we took my not-so-dirty tee shirts and put the pillows in them, then decided to sleep in our cloths. That would get us through the day and night until we could get back on the plane — or so we thought.

We lay down and I dreamt there was a mouse standing on my chest. Being in a dream state, I jumped up and screamed at the top of my lungs, "There's a mouse, there's a mouse." I finally realized I wasn't afraid of mice and not dreaming. I was actually jumping up and down on the bed with the mouse bouncing next to me.

Darlene jumped off the bed and dove across the floor; sliding on her stomach into the bathroom. I collapsed on the bed, sweating from head to foot. I did not see where the mouse went. But I was sure he would think twice about getting on my chest again.

I laid down again. A few minutes later, I hear a distant soft and whimpering little voice call to me. "Happy anniversary honey." The *honey* part was real soft. Yes! It was our anniversary. One year from the day we tied the knot in Coeur d'Alene.

Just minutes after I fell to the bed and heard Darlene, the room exploded with the sound of three tiny little men pounding on the door for all they were worth trying to find out what had happened to us.

We regrouped and managed a couple hours sleep. When we got our wits about us, we counted our money and chose to spend a little on a chicken sandwich and a coke. I peeked out of our room and placed an order with a little Indian man standing in the hall.

An hour later, he opened the door and walked in without knocking. We paid our Rupees and sat on the bed to partake of the feast. I removed the napkin to find what looked like a cupcake. I picked it up. It felt cool and weighed heavy. I thought, *Well, I guess it is a chicken sandwich after all — just a little different shape.*

I bit into it and quickly got a very *not-chicken* taste in my mouth. I looked in my hand at what I had just bitten into. It was looking back at me. I spit out that strange tasting goo and grabbed the Coke. It was warm and flat and very sweet. I fell back on the bed and watched the ceiling fan rotate, trying get a grip on what was happening. Darlene opened the door and asked about ice for our drink and got a big-eyed stare from the little Indian fellow.

India wasn't where we wanted to be. I pulled out the United Airlines itinerary and came to the forgotten realization that the airline only flew into New Deli every other day. Plus, we could only fly sand-by. Horror of horrors, we had to spend another day here.

We didn't have enough money for another night in this 1-star inn and a suitable meal. We rested up, checked out at noon the next day and went to the airport to wait for our flight at 4:30 the next morning. We thought we might find a decent meal in the airport, but it had to be cheap. We now had less than $20. Since they fed us on the plane, we knew we could hold on that long.

We found seats at the airport and settled in for a long wait. We played a lot of Canasta on the trip to keep our minds sharp; we had something to do. The food in the airport proved to not be much better than the hotel. We found that the cashews were very big and wonderful. Darlene liked the S-flavored milk sold in Coca Cola bottles from one of those old five-cent chest coolers. S-flavored milk is cow's milk mixed with pineapple juice. She liked it, but I wasn't that desperate.

I got restless after a while and took a stroll around the airport. I found the men's room and went in to check it out. Sitting in the corner were three ladies cooking food and smoking pot. I used the facilities and when I tried to leave, they demanded a Rupee. I thought that was a little much and started investigating further. I walked to the other end of the building and found there was a better class section. I thought we should move down there.

I went back to Darlene and told her the news. But when I gathered our stuff, I heard that small still voice telling me to stay in the seats we had. Great, now I was stuck with the poor people. Just before the plane arrived, I went to the check in counter and discovered we needed $10 each for the airport tax. I lost hope of getting out of this place and went over to break the news to Darlene. I plopped in the chair and set myself to figure out what we were to do. We had enough money for one of us to get out of the country but not both of us.

We decided to pray. I know that's an obvious solution. But we were worn out. We stayed in our seats like I was told we should and waited. The plane we would use to depart on landed. The disembarking passengers passed us while we sat waiting. An American family from California sat next to us. They said they were having a problem with their luggage; somehow, oil was spilled on their bags. We talked for some time. And when they got up to leave, the man of the family handed me his business card. Attached to the back of it was a $20 bill. Thank you, Jesus!

Salem

We landed back home at the San Francisco airport and called my folks. They picked us up and took us to their home in Santa Cruz, California. Where we spent time getting reacclimated and helping my folks with projects around the house.

We borrowed their motor home and spent a couple of weeks in Napa Valley; my old stopping grounds. Napa didn't work for us. So we headed back to Santa Cruz and talked about where we would get are lives started again.

We decided Salem, Oregon was where we would like to live. We had a standing invitation from Larry Turner to be part of the church, and he would help us get established. We gave him a call.

We prayed, asking the Lord to find jobs for both of us. If that happened, we would know Salem was where he wanted us. In one day, we both had jobs with a company in West Salem; a businessman in Larry's Church. We moved our stuff to Salem, found an apartment and settled in.

STEAK

While living and serving at the church in Salem, Oregon, Darlene and I found ourselves short of funds. After returning to the USA from our trip around the world, I had taken a minimum wage job to try and make ends meet.

Well, the ends met but there was no meat left to eat. I moaned one day after eating another bowl of oatmeal. I declared that I just had to have a good steak or I would have a fit. Darlene let me know that she only had $3 and that I was not going to have it.

I was not deterred by her lack of obedience. After all, I was the leader in the home. I repeated my desire for some hot meat, but to no avail. I still did not get her $3.

I decided to take this to a higher authority and told her, "God wants to meet this need!" I continued saying, "I will just have to go where the meat is." She said I was crazy!

I got in my car and drove to Roth's IGA in West Salem, without the $3. It was still morning, around 9 AM, when I entered the store. They had just waxed their shiny white floors and the store was fairly empty. So, I strolled confidently to the meat department and found my way to the porterhouse steaks. I dug around until I could find the best steak.

I made sure there was enough so Darlene could share the bounty. The label said $9.95. I swallowed a few times to keep from drooling on the clean floors.

I looked around to make sure no one was in earshot. And holding the steak above my head, I proclaimed, "Okay God. You said you would provide for me according to your riches in Glory. So, here I am."

A very clear voice spoke to my spirit and said, "Look Down!" I was standing on a $10 bill.

China Trip #1

In 1999, I invented and patented a woodworking tool. At the National Hardware show in Chicago in 2000, the tool won the "Best New Tool of The Year" award. It made the covers of many magazines, written up in the Chicago Tribune and mentioned on Good Morning America.

While at the Chicago show, I had Lunch with businessman from Taiwan. Mister Chow gave me his business card and mentioned he was building a new factory in Foshon. After he had left the table, I wrote on the edge of the card the name of a city he mentioned: Foshon. I did not think much about it, at the time.

As he turned and walked away, I heard God say very clearly, "Knock yourself off before they knock you off!" I was warned that the Chinese came to shows, took good ideas back to China and reproduced them. The Lord was warning me about this and telling me what I needed to do.

When I came home from Chicago, I talked with my business partner about what I had heard from the Lord. He agreed that we needed to take action. I got on the Internet and investigated several aluminum extruders in Guangzhou, southern China. I told them I would call when I got there. I made a list of three contacts in China and set it on my desk. I got my passport and visa, then hopped on a plane to Hong Kong.

Arriving in Hong Kong airport and suffering jet-lag, I did not know which way to go. I noticed a Chinese man watching me walk around the airport. I went over to confront this nosy guy. As I approached him he said, "Are you going to Guangzhou?" I said sure and he said, "I will take you, follow me." This Chinese man was from Canada and headed for a trade show 100 miles into the mainland. This was really cool, as I had not told any of my contacts in China when I was coming. So I thought this guy was an angel sent to help me.

We took the high-speed train from the airport into Hong Kong and entered another large train station. The place was packed. I had felt the Lord wanted me in Guangzhou at noon. Although I couldn't remember why, it sounded good to me.

We went to the window to purchase our tickets. The lady behind the glass told us the next available seats would be on the 2:30 train. It was 8 in the morning, and I could not wait that long. My Chinese partner and I walked across the station and he suggested we take a bus. I said, "No that would be just as crowded." When I said that, I looked back toward the lady at the ticket counter and saw her jumping up and down waving in our direction. We made our way back to see what the fuss was all about. On the way, a man offered us two tickets for $100 each, US. I shook my head and kept going to the ticket counter. When we arrived there was a little, thin man standing next to the counter with two tickets for the 9:30 train. He only wanted $15 each; just what they cost him. Cool stuff, eh?

We settled in on the train and passed through customs into the mainland. I opened my briefcase to look at my contact list. Wouldn't you know? I left the list on my office desk in Vancouver, in the good old USA. Great! Now here I was in mainland China with nowhere to go.

I searched my briefcase more thoroughly. I pulled everything out. Digging behind my own business cards, I came up with the card I got from Mister Chow at Chicago's trade show. I showed it to the man from Canada and we noticed the city name Foshon written on the side of the card. I wrote it on the card while in Chicago. At the same time we looked at the card, I glanced out the window of the train as a sign for Foshon flashed by. I remembered from the train schedule in the station that this was the only train that stopped in Foshon that day. Then another sign for Foshon flashed past the window.

The train was slowing for the Foshon station stop. I turned to the man I was with and pointed to the word Foshon written on its side. The man simply said, "Get off the train." I had not noticed that Mister Chow's business card address was on Taiwan. Taiwan was a thousand miles away.

I got off the train, walked through the station and out the front entrance. Then I ran back in. About a hundred beggars accosted me.

I stood inside the train station looking out at the masses. I wondered, then I wondered some more. I looked back at the business card in my hand and was surprised to see a cell number at the bottom. I considered doubtfully what good it would be. But, it was worth a try. I talked to a lady behind a desk and pointed to the cell number on the card. I gave her some money and she called the number.

Mister Chow answered. He said abruptly, "Who is this? I am on the other line and can't talk to you."

I said, "Hi Sammy, this is Jack Schooley."

He said, "Who? I don't know you!"

I said, "Remember Chicago? The level I invented?"

"Jack! Why you call me?"

"Sammy! I am here to get my level made."

"Jack! I am headed for Taiwan I cannot help you."

I said, "That was fine. Could you find me someone that can help me?"

He said, "Where are you now?"

I said, "I am at the Foshon train station."

There was a gasp then a short silence. Then he said, "You are not going to believe this. But I am driving right in front of that train station now!"

I was in the car within ten minutes. Sammy took me to Guangzhou and introduced me to a manufacturer that could help me with my level. I visited their factory and had a good time seeing China. At the end of the day, I was deposited in the Jindui hotel in Foshon. And with that came four days with nothing to do.

After checking in and getting settled in my room, I came down to the lobby and checked out all the Chinese artwork. I was getting hungry but did not know how to find a place to eat, let alone order from a menu. I spotted a Chinese man sleeping on a leather couch in the lobby. I walked over, sat down.

"Hi," I said. "Do I know you?"

He sat up and said in perfect English, "No, I don't think so. But sit down and we can talk."

I did so. And after a cordial exchange, he informed me that he would pick up his business partner and return in an hour. They would take me out for dinner.

An hour later I returned to the leather couch in the lobby to meet my new friends. I was only there a few minutes when they walked in. This handsome young man that I had met while he slept on the leather couch, introduced me to his business partner.

He said, "Paulman, this is Jack Schooley." Paulman backed up and uttered in an excited voice, "This must be God!"

Paulman was the most important contact I had on my list. I had been emailing him for three months. My list was still on the desk 7,000 miles away! It is wonderful how God works. Not just sometimes, but all the time.

Gary was the name of the man asleep on the couch. Chris told me some months later how Gary came to be on that couch at the Jindui hotel. Chris was a driver for a large aluminum extruder in the Nanhai City industrial area. Chris and Gary are friends and were going out for dinner that night. On the way, Chris got a phone call from his boss, the owner of Silver One Hundred. The owner of the company asked Chris to come to his home, get him and drive him to a restaurant for dinner. Chris had to do something with Gary, so he dropped him at the Jindui hotel. When Chris drove to his boss' home to pick him up, the boss came to the door and asked, "Why are you here?

Chris said, "You called me to come.

The boss said, "I did not call you. You go," and closed the door.

Apparently, Jesus has a cell phone.

Chris is an underground Christian and the first one to take us to a church in China.

China Trip #2

Prophecy over Dali, China

On my next trip to China I was met at the Hong Kong airport by my new business partners. They showed me Hong Kong and took me into mainland China where we set up our factory.

I was put in an eighth-floor room in one of the tallest hotels in Dali; a town close to our factory. I settled in for the night. But, about 3 AM I woke with a start. I jumped out of bed and threw open the curtains and looked into complete darkness. There was not a light on in this large city.

I said, "This place is really dark."

When I said that, I heard the Lord say to me, "Then speak against that darkness."

I said something like, "Lord, I ask you to send your warring angels to this city and set your people free."

I closed the drapes, went back to bed and fell asleep just after thinking how crazy I was.

Two years later I was resting in a hotel in Shanghai, feeling sorry for myself. I was having a little pity-party and feeling like I never got to do anything fun.

While I lay there in this frump a voice says to me, "Remember Dali?" I perked up and rolled my eyes a little trying to get the right picture. I had just flown to Shanghai from Dali a few days before. I pictured what Dali was like on my last visit. They had just finished paving the streets and putting in streetlights. The old corrupt city government was thrown out and the people could now walk the streets without fear. The whole town was changed for the better.

After going over this list of changes the Lord had brought to Dali, I thought, "Lord, I can't take credit for any of that."

He responded, "That is true."

China #3

Nancy

On my next trip I realized I would have to hire my own assistant interpreter. Paulman put out the word to the local employment agency and I interviewed three new interpreters.

After interviewing them I chose a young lady named Nancy. She had a university degree, her English was the best of all three, and she had some experience working for her father's factory.

On the second interview, I told Nancy she had the job and I would like her to come and stay at the hotel so I could spend the next 3 days training her in all the aspects of the job.

Nancy got up from where she was sitting in the office, walked out the door and headed up the street. I was shocked to say the least. I ran back into the factory to find Paulman. I found him eating a bowl of rice out in back. I told him that Nancy had hit the road and I did not know why.

Paulman took out his cell phone and called her. He spoke to her in Chinese so I did not understand what was being said. They talked for some time. When he hung up and put his phone back on his belt, he started eating again and mumbled through his rice, "She will come back."

I asked, "What Happened?"

He mumbled, "She thought you wanted her to stay with you at the hotel."

Now I understood a little more about communications in China. Nancy has high moral values. That evening I took a taxi to meet Nancy's family and then we checked her into a room at the hotel across from mine.

The next morning, Nancy called my room and I told her to meet me for breakfast in the lobby. We spent the next two day's going over her responsibilities in the factory and designing quality control manuals for her to operate out of.

That afternoon we were a little tired of work so I asked Nancy if I could go to her home village and visit the kindergarten her mother operated. We stopped and bought candy for the little ones. When we arrived, I went in and sat on a little stool. These wonderful little girls came out and did their Chinese twirling dances for me. I rewarded them all with little bags of M&Ms. That was a great time.

That evening Nancy was in her room and I was watching Pearl, the English television station sent on cable into southern China. I heard this knock on my door and I opened to see Nancy with her head hung very low. I told her she could come in and she slowly walked into the room. I had left the door open so she would feel comfortable, sat down and asked her if something was troubling her.

She began to weep, got up on the end of my bed and crossed her legs like the Indians do, then held up her foot and pointed at her big toe. She sniffed a little and said, "My father has never seen this toe before."

What struck me the most about this bazaar situation was how bad her feet smelled. More than that, they really stunk bad. I was at the point of crying for that reason alone. Well, I held it together and continued to listen to this sad little girl. What Nancy said next really touched my heart.

"When I was just a little girl; like the ones you love at the kindergarten; I dropped a board on my toe and broke the nail here. And it has never grown right from that time on."

I let go of my nose at that and realized something profound was happening in Nancy's heart and I wanted to enjoy it also.

She continued, "I saw you love those little ones at the kindergarten and enjoy them. When I hurt this toe my father did not want to see it. And he never told me he loved me and I have always wanted him to love me."

She paused and I said, "I love you like you were my only daughter." I reached out and took hold of that smelly toe and said, "I love this toe and I am so sorry you have had such a disappointing relationship with your father."

Nancy hung her head then said, "Could you be my father?"

I said, "I will love you like the father I know loves me. He has a son Named Jesus Christ that has come to help us love one another. Let me tell you about him."

Later, I took Nancy into the bathroom, ran the tub half full of warm water and washed her feet. That really cemented our relationship.

The next morning, I met Nancy in the lobby and asked her if we could find a restaurant that served American food. We set out to find one and only walked around the block when we saw a Taiwanese restaurant on the corner. We went in to look at the menu and lo and behold, there it was — waffles. Praise God, real food.

We sat down and I told Nancy I was going to order her a real American breakfast. She asked the waitress for me if they had butter. It took some time to explain to Nancy what butter was because they just don't use it in southern China. We also discovered they had strawberry jam, but no syrup. But we were on a roll and it was still going to be a treat.

The waffles came. I put butter and jam on them and handed it across to Nancy. She cut herself a bite and began to chew. Her eyes got real big and rolled back in her head. She began to moan. "Oh! Oh! How wonderful. Oh! Oh! I have never tasted so good!" She smacked her lips over and over again.

That evening, there was this little knock on my door. Nancy came strutting in closing the door behind her. She jumped up on the bed and crossed her legs like the Indians. I was reading my brand-new leather-bound Bible. I had bought it just for this trip. I read some to Nancy and we talked about it for some time. We prayed together and talked about me leaving the next day.

Then it happened! The Lord said to me, "Give her your new Bible." Ouch! I thought, this is the Bible I have always wanted and I just love it and I don't want to! My next thought was, you bring a Bible to China and then you take it away. I bit my lip, looked up at Nancy and said very quietly, "Would you like to have the Word of God?" I extended my beautiful, leather-bound new Bible to her.

Her mouth fell open and she began to smack her lips over and over again just like she did over the waffles that morning. It was as if she could taste the Word of God. She took it slowly, prying it out of my hands, and put it to her breast and covering it with both hands. Now tears were streaming now down both our faces.

I left the next day a happy man.

China #3

Jo and the Bamboo

After some trips, back and forth to China, I realized I would have to spend a lot more of my time getting the factory up and rolling. I packed up my wife and moved her to China with me.

We found a nice little place, not far from the factory and set ourselves up a home. Darlene needed a housekeeper and companion to look after her.

One day we drove over to Dali to do some shopping at a nice little market. As we wandered through the little market we were having some difficulty. Since we did not have an interpreter with us, we could not tell what was in the packages.

After some exasperation, a young Chinese girl who was working in the Market came over and said, "Can I help you?"

"Yes!" my wife and I said in unison.

This was Jo! She was so charming and bubbly we liked her from the start. We paid for our stuff and left, heading back to our home in Lishui. On the trip back, Paulman was driving us. I turned to him and said, "Do you think you could get that little girl to come and work for us and be Darlene's helper?"

Paulman said he would look into it.

After a day or two Paulman shows up at out home with Jo in tow. She agreed to work for us, living in our home.

It was not long until Darlene had smothered Jo with her motherly love and led this wonderful girl to the Lord. I can't remember exactly when Jo mentioned that the Lord spoke to her when we met her in the market. That she would come and help us live in China. She certainly was a great help.

Her whole family became our family and her 93 years young grandmother became such a love to me. When I could, I would go visit her with Jo and take them out for lunch. This beautiful woman lived her life in the same home when she died. In 1939 the Japanese came and took the doors and windows out of her mud hut and built fires to cook their rice on. I will miss our times together.

Darlene and I went out and bought some wonderful furniture for our home. One day I was looking at the wall and thought they needed pictures. Darlene had left for the US a few days before, so I had the task of buying wall hangings myself.

Jo took me to Guangzhou to a market for Chinese art. We found suitable pieces and headed home.

Well, it turns out the walls in the home were made of cement and I was not interested in driving nails into cement. So, I decided to get a long bamboo pole to hang them from. This way I only had to drive two nails instead of four.

After Jo arrived at our home the next day, we got in my little car and headed out to the country to find bamboo. We just passed through a little village when we saw a bamboo thicket behind a small mud hut. I pulled over and Jo and I hiked to the hut. Jo called out to the little hut and a young boy, all sleepy eyed, came out in his raged cloths. Jo asked if we could cut a Bamboo pole and he didn't seem to think there would be any problem, even though he was home alone; his mother and father where away working in the fields. He led the way and we selected a fine pole. I cut it down and we drug it back and fastened it to the side of the car.

While I was tying it on, Jo disappeared into the mud hut with the boy. Though she was only gone for a moment, I heard the Lord speak to me. He said, "I will talk to Jo. I will tell her to give the boy $100RMB."

Jo returned from the mud hut a few minutes later and her face was as red as her little brown face could possibly be. She just looked at me, but could not talk. I finally just smiled at the sweet little thing and said, "The Lord has just spoken to you, yes?" Jo's mouth dropped open and she just nodded her head up and down.

I went on and said," The Lord said to you, "give the boy $100RMB, yes?" Jo started to cry as I reached in my pocket to fish out the money.

Jo found her voice and said, "I was so afraid, I did not know what you would say if I asked to do this. I will pay you back when we get home."

I said, "No Jo. It is my pleasure, also."

China #5

Provision

All things did not work out for our little adventure in China. We had a hard time getting a vital part for the products we were building. Additionally, the quality was not good enough for US standards. By the time we got it figured out, we ran out of money.

I got the call one day from my business partner, a truly wonderful brother in the Lord, and he said, in so many words, "It is over. I have to stop the bleeding and shut the company down — you are on your own."

I called my wife, who had moved back to the USA, and let her know I would be coming home. We were in shock. All our hopes and dreams in China, and our own material success — scuttled.

What would we do? We had mounds of dept and our cash cow had just broken its leg and died on us. I flew home, not knowing what would happen.

I was home for not too long when this man of God I had met called and said he had some people he wanted me to meet.

I arrived at his home at the scheduled time. He asked me to share my testimony of what had proceeded in China and I told our story. After I had finished, they said they would like to give me one hundred dollars to help with my mission. I was flattered that they wanted to help. But I asked them to wait on the Lord over the weekend and let me know if they still wanting to do this. A hundred bucks is a lot of money.

The next Monday, we met for lunch to chat some more. And they handed me checks totaling $100,000 US. They gave it as an offering. No strings attached. We paid off our bills and I continued my work in China doing consulting and product development for other companies.

Back in the USA

Larry Turner

I had built an apartment on the back of our home for my mother to live in until she passed away. We kept the apartment for us to come home to while we were in the USA. When Darlene moved to China to be with me, we rented our apartment to a friend.

After Darlene came home due to health issues, she moved into the big house and the apartment lay vacant; using just some of it for an office.

We got a call from friends telling us Larry Turner was having health and financial problems. Larry was a music Pastor friend of ours that we served with in Salem, OR, way back in the early 80's. We felt lead to call Larry and offer our studio apartment to him for as long as he needed it; free of charge. Larry jumped at the offer and said he would be coming up from California very soon. We cleaned it out and waited.

Larry showed one day and settled in.

Larry knew everyone in the music industry. It did not matter who you mentioned, or who was on TV, Larry knew them. Some of the biggest names in Christian gospel would send Larry cassettes of their recordings, so he could write arrangements for them. Larry was a well-known artist in his own right.

On one occasion Larry asked us to accompany him to Albany, Oregon. He said there was a wonderful revival going on was determined to make the trip every day. We wanted to be in on the blessing, so I offered to drive taking him and Darlene.

The worship was wonderful, and the message was well inspired. It was about halfway through the message and when something started. As they say in prophetic circles, I was reading people's mail that sat in front of us. It was a mother and her three daughters. I tapped each one on the shoulder and told them what God was going to do in their lives and how much He loved them. Afterwards they came and said I had hit all their callings right on the mark. That was cool.

Afterward, my hands began to burn and sting. It felt like someone was driving nails in them. I reached over and laid my hands on Darlene and she jumped and said, "your hands feel so hot!"

Larry leaned over and I told him what was happening and he said, "I knew Catherine Kuhlman's assistant and she had the same thing in her hands. She was the prayer power behind Catherine Kuhlman."

This stinging in the palms of my hands has stayed with me through the years. When the Holy Spirit is moving my hands feel like there are nails being driven in them. They sting but it has never been a bother, just a wonderful blessing.

After the service was over, Darlene and Larry went up for prayer and I stayed in my seat nursing my swollen red hands. I was uncomfortable with all this; I had never heard of such a thing and probably would have not believed it if someone had told me they had experienced it as a sign from the Lord. While I was seated there, I watched a man across the sanctuary. He kept looking at me as he worked through the chairs and people lying on the floor.

After a few minutes he had found his way over and sat next to me. We exchanged cordialities and then he said, "The Lord is telling me I need you to pray for my wife and me. We are leaving for China to adopt an orphan on September 6th."

I just sat there looking at my hands thinking about what to pray. I can't remember what I said, but I was a little in shock due to my hands burning and I too was leaving on September 6th for China.

The Lord was telling me, the cross of Jesus Christ was for China and that was my purpose. To take his sacrifice to the Chinese people and he gave me this sign, in my flesh, to keep me on the path.

Back on the home front, dear Larry was not doing well. The Lord had told me that Larry was coming to our home to stay until he died.

Larry had this habit of leaving all the doors open, including our garage door. He was so irresponsible sometimes that we felt we could not leave him to take care of things when we were in China. We both were leaving to go back for an extended time, so we were compelled to take it to the Lord.

About 10:30 one night Darlene and I lay in bed discussing this problem. I prayed, "Lord, we love Larry, but we can't leave him here alone, so maybe it is time to take him home or find him a new home."

I lay there after praying waiting to drift off to sleep. I was facing the clock next to my bed and it said eleven o'clock. I heard the garage door open and Larry entered his apartment. In just a few seconds I heard what would turn out to be Larry's last gasp of breath. Then I fell asleep.

The next morning, I knew what had happened. I rolled over and said to Darlene, "I think Larry passed away last night. I am going out to check on him."

When I opened my back door, Larry's apartment door stood open and I could see Larry's feet. I called to him, but there was no response, so I walked in and sure enough, there was Larry, half smiling, on his back across the bed and the garage door open.

Larry is undoubtedly leaving doors open in heaven.

Ford Ranger

The Mechanics of Faith

One Sunday, I packed my little three-cylinder Chinese automobile full of friends and headed off to Shamion Island for church.

Among other things, Shamion Island is the main processing point in China for adopting Chinese babies. The American embassy is there and the most fortunate parents have the blessing of staying in the White Swan Hotel; a real beautiful place with waterfalls and koi fish swimming about in pools.

We arrived early at the church and found seats halfway toward the front.

About halfway through the service I got the impression I was to get up and go outside. I climbed my way over the people in the Pews and stepped carefully around the ones camped in the isles. When I got outside I found an American lady with pretty blond hair holding the most adorable little baby girl. I said to the lady, "That is one beautiful child. You are so blessed and so is the child."

The Lady thanked me then formed a serious look on her face. "What are you doing in China?"

I said, "I am in manufacturing."

She told me when she left her church in Texas the previous Sunday, a man named Robin King said to her, "If you find an American doing manufacturing in China, I need to contact him."

I wrote down her email address and when I got home to Lishui, I sent her an email right away knowing she would not get it for some time. Three months later I received an email from Robin King of Comfort, Texas. Robin is a true man of God and I have traveled for him in China and flown down to be with his wonderful family several times.

Robin asked me if I would like to do some work for his company based in Del Rio, Texas. He also stated I could work from home. I liked that idea and took the offer. He told me to fly down to Texas and stay with them for a while and learn the business. So began the Mechanics of Faith.

In March of 2005 a funny thing happened on the way to San Antonio!

Darlene and I decided I should drive instead of fly, even though I could fly for free. I knew the trip would be three days of hard driving. My main concern was I would be driving my 1990 Ford Ranger Pickup. It had 172,000 miles on it. A thought kept going through my mind, "What if the transmission goes out?" Another automatic transmission ran between $1,200 and $1,600 big ones in those days.

I hit the road very early Tuesday morning. Everything went well; I was really enjoying the time alone and the weather was wonderful. My sweet little Ranger was running flat out; just a tad over the legal limit to keep up with traffic at three in the morning.

On the 2nd day I got a call from my Robin asking me to stop by Roswell, New Mexico and check out an equipment auction. I was happy to do this for him. I have always wanted to meet up with some of them aliens down in Roswell. Of course, I do that regularly every Sunday at church.

About 3:30 that afternoon I headed up the grade east of Albuquerque. I noticed my tachometer going up, but my speed was not. Yes, you guessed it; the automatic transmission was slipping. The first thought that popped into my head was not thank you Jesus. It was holly crap!
!
Well, this was the beginning of my search for "The Mechanics Faith". I kept driving for another hour until I found a service station. I needed gas anyway. When I stopped, I pulled the transmission dipstick on my poor little pickup. The transmission had plenty of fluid. The problem was it was black instead of red and didn't smell good. I knew what that meant; my transmission did not shift anymore because it had burned up.

So now, what was the wise thing to do? Wisdom would turn around and drive the one and a half hours back to Albuquerque and get the transmission fixed.

What came from my lips was, "Lord, you sent me to San

Antonio, and I am not turning back!"

I picked my teeth over that a few minutes and decided I would take the turnoff to Roswell and see what would happen next. I looked at my cell phone and found there were no bars showing; no cell phone service. Then I looked down the road at the darkening sky with its thunder and lightning. Flash flood signs along the road suggested I might be heading for trouble.

From the gas station to Roswell there would be 140 miles with no service stations, stores or anything else — that is why aliens like it there so much. I kept my speed at 55 miles an hour. It wasn't long before it was completely dark. Hail made a terrible racket on my poor little Ranger's windshield. I had simultaneously been working my faith for an hour and a half after discovering the transmission problem near Albuquerque. I had gone through all the tools of faith that I knew to use; praying in the spirit and all that. But the transmission was still slipping.

Finally, I took my stand and said, "Lord you told me to go to Texas and I am going. I have a blanket and a pillow in the back of this truck and if you don't fix this transmission, I will crawl in the back of the truck lay down and stay there until you fix it, but I am not turning back!"

I can't remember how long it took; maybe two to five minutes; and the transmission shifted into high gear. Myself and little Ranger were off to the races for the next 800 miles.

To tell you the truth I may have faith, but I am not stupid. Although that idea may be up for debate, when I arrived at my friend's home in Texas I asked if he knew a good transmission guy. He sent me to his brother-in-law who had a garage just down the street. I dropped my sweet little truck off and told him my testimony of what had happened the day before.

The next day I walked down to get my truck and they looked me right in the eye and said, "There was not a bit of dirt, or sludge and the filters in the transmission were perfectly clean." He said there was no burned smell to the oil, and the oil and transmission were just like new.

I think my Mechanic did a real fine job. To date, I have put 60,000 miles on that Holy Spirit transmission.

Mary Going to Heaven

My mother; whose name is Mary; lived in the apartment I built for her on the back of our house for a couple of years. She and I always had fun together hiking, backpacking, canoeing and fishing.

When she was too old to take care of herself, she wanted to be in an adult care facility. She didn't want her son changing her diapers. Every week or two for about a year I would drive over in her favorite car; my Eldorado Cadillac; and take a drive up the Columbia River gorge.

We stopped near the Bonneville Dam and got burgers, then take them to the park and watch the Canadian geese graze on the grass. Every time she saw the geese, she would comment, "When I die, I hope the Lord will let me experience what it is like to fly, swim and travel all over the world. I want to experience what it would be like to be a Canadian goose."

I always told her that would be nice, followed by a smile.

Early one morning the care facility called to let us know my mom had passed away. After I said thanks and hung up, Darlene rolled over and asked, "Is your mom gone?"

We had lay there quietly for a few minutes when we heard the wings of a gaggle of geese beating low over the house. One of the geese kept honking hello.

In twenty years of living in our home, it was the only time that had happened. Darlene and I never shed a tear for my mother. Only Jesus knows what she is doing now.

A Trip to Beijing

I woke one morning at the beginning of August in 2003 with the Lord's voice saying, "Go to the communist government headquarters in Beijing and tell them to let my people go."

I responded with, "Right! I read a story like that in the Bible. That's crazy and I'm not going to do it."

I put my pillow over my face, assuring myself I was nuts and tried to go back to sleep. I lay there for some time while deciding to create some event to prove once and for all I was crazy.

"So," I said, "to whomever that voice was that had been speaking to me, if you want me to go to Beijing, you will have to have my wife tell me, 'I want to go to Beijing.' And I won't give you any help with this. I will keep my mouth shut."

I had read this story and had no idea what good would come

of this crazy idea. It didn't take long for me to forget about the incident.

Three days later, my wife and I were standing in the bedroom. With her birthday coming up on the twenty-fifth of September, I probed, "Honey what would you like for your birthday?"

She enthusiastically blurted out, "I want to go to Beijing!"

Shocked and scared, I blurted back, "I am not going. I don't want go there!"

She reacted, "Oh, I just got to go!"

I sat her on the couch and told her what I was told to do. She said I was crazy, but she still wanted to go. "So, you want me to make the reservations?" She insisted that I should.

We went to our house church a few days later and told them what the Lord said to me. They got excited about the idea, put me in a chair and anointed me with oil. As they were prayed, Bill Peterson our leader, said he had a word from the Lord.

He prophesied that God would anoint my feet with oil. It was a comforting and encouraging word. Then he handed me a large bottle of anointing oil to put in my pocket.

On the fourteenth of October, Darlene and I left for Beijing. We checked into a nice hotel and the next day took a tour of the city. After four hours of a grueling tour of old buildings in a tour bus was weaving its way through back streets, the bus stopped. The tour guide jumped to his feet and looked at us. He pointed to a tall cement wall with a gate. A soldier with a big gun stood in front of it. The guide said, "This is the real government headquarters," then sat down.

I looked at Darlene. She rolled her eyes and just shook her head. The look on her face said I was crazy. Standing in front of that gated entrance to the compound was tall Chinese solder with a .50 caliber Gatling Gun in his arms. I understood.

For the next two to three hours, we drove around to hotels dropping off tour people. Being the last ones on the bus, we ended at our hotel. It was dark and we were totally worn out.

In the morning, my wife was sick with a migraine headache. I knew what I was about to do would be an all-day event. I asked her what she wanted. She responded, "Turn the light out and go do your thing."

I grabbed the anointing oil and went down to the lobby. Then standing in front of the hotel wondering which way was north, which way was south and where in the world this government headquarters was. Since we had driven around and around the city and I simply did not have a clue about where to find the HQ in a city of thirteen and a half million people.

A taxi rolled up to the curb. I had the doorman tell him to take me to the Beijing hotel. I figured that would be in the center of the city and I could go from there. When we got to the Beijing hotel I went inside and asked, "Where is the government headquarters?"

The girl looked at me funny and pointed out the front door. I walked out front and kept going. I was sure I could find this needle in a haystack. I crossed a six-lane street and walked for a half hour. I turned a corner and found myself at the exact spot where the tour driver said, "this is the real government headquarters." I remembered the trees and the color of the high walls lining the street. A different soldier at the gate with the same machine gun and the red flag was a good indication of the fact.

I waved at the soldier with the gun and said hello. He didn't say anything and shifted the machine gun in my direction. I gave him my most friendly look — to no avail.

I did not know how I was going to get in there and see the right people. As I stood there wondering, a thought came to me. "Just pray for them. Our warfare is not against flesh and blood."

This was great! Now I was off the hook. I could do this. I reached for the bottle of anointing oil in my pocket. I opened it, put some on my finger, then wiped it on the tall barbed wire covered wall. The guard did not like that. He turned to me, with a very unpleasant glair on his face. So, I headed for the corner to get out of site.

As I got around the corner, it felt like I had a rock in my shoe. I reached down and stuck my finger inside of my tennis shoe to extract the rock. I forgot I had the bottle of oil in my hand with the lid off. When I bent over, I proceeded to pour all of the oil over my shoe and hand.

The word Bill had given me was, "I will anoint your feet with oil." I had the ROCK in my shoe and now my feet were anointed with oil! A prophetic picture. Go figure.

At the time, I just thought I made a big mess. My hands were covered with oil and now every step I took had a footprint of oil. So, I wiped my hand on the walls as I prayed my way around the HQ. That took about forty minutes. I kept wiping and walking and praying, "Lord, cover them with your presence and send your angels to protect those in here from the powers of darkness, and let my people go."

When I finished, my hands were still covered with oil. I made my way back to the Beijing hotel and washed up. Then I grabbed a taxi back to my hotel to meet up with my wife.

Two weeks passed after arriving home from China, when I got a call from a pastor friend. He an outreach into Mainland China. We met for lunch and I told him about my Beijing trip. He was very moved and encouraged, then confided in me he recently flew to Hong Kong to meet associates. Afterward off to Beijing. He was put in the trunk of a car and smuggled into the government headquarters. He and his friends were led to the number three leader in the government of China, who was in charge of all religion. He knew the Lord, was Spirit-filled and lived at the headquarters I had covered in prayer.

Two weeks after my lunch with this pastor, the Chinese Government changed laws allowing all underground churches to come out and worship openly.

Gold Teeth and the

Salvation of Winnie the Pooh

I woke up Passover morning sometime back, crawled out of bed and headed to the bathroom. This morning was laid back with no plans to do anything — until I started brushing my teeth. I put the toothpaste on the brush and started brushing. I spotted a gleam in my mouth and pulled my cheek back. And there it was — a gold tooth!

I stood there shocked. Had I forgotten I had one? I rinsed the toothpaste from my mouth and called to my wife; she never forgets anything. "Honey, do I have a gold tooth?"

She called back, "No, you don't."

I had heard testimonies out of Argentina and all the stuff about supernatural dental work. But at the time this happened, I was not convinced gold fillings and teeth were really happening. I thought they might be mere stories.

I went to the kitchen, pulled my cheek back and questioned, "Then, what is this?"

She got quiet, but I could hear gears turning. She said, "You better call your dentist."

We had the same dentist for several years. I felt the freedom to call and ask him to get out my file. He came back on the phone and said he had retrieved my file. I asked him point blank, "Do I have a gold tooth?" I heard pages turning, then he cleared his throat and said, "Nope! No gold tooth."

I went to Clark Collage dental school and had the professor of dentistry look at it. He asked, "Where did you get that tooth?"

"I woke up Passover morning and it was there," I responded.

"I have never seen a tooth like that." Walking away shaking his head, he mumbled, "No man could make a tooth like that."

When I got home, I ran up and down the street in front of my house wondering what to do. My neighbors had to think I was crazy.

Darlene and I had been going to Bethel Church in Redding, California once every month or two — 420 miles each way. That was the only place I could think of to go and show my gold tooth. They should not be too surprised.

We packed up and headed for Bethel. Dropping Darlene off at her sister's in Roseburg, Oregon, I continued to Redding. They were having a conference so I could only sit in the coffee shop and show my tooth.

The next day, I was strolling about the deck on the outside of the church and noticed a sweet little Asian girl chatting at a table. I sat down at their table and showed them my gold tooth. They were very excited and we became friends right off.

That night at the church was an open worship time. I was excited be a part of it. The room was crowded and everyone was jumping and dancing around. I walked to the front to participate in the action. I reached out and touched two worshipers; they hit the floor, slain in the spirit. I turned around, staggering and headed for the back.

A woman in her forties jumped out and grabbed my arm. She looked me in the eye and said, "I perceive you are a prophet of the Lord and you have something to impart to me."

I held my cupped hands in front of me and replied, "Put your heart in my hands. Whatever you put in my hands will be done unto you."

She hugged me and shared her heart's desire. I remember it like it was today. What she told me was like reading my own heart; we had the same heart.

She stopped and pushed me back and said, "You aren't going to believe this, but on Passover morning I woke up, went to the bathroom to brush my teeth, and I had a new gold tooth."

"Like this?" Showing her the gold tooth in my mouth.

As you can imagine, I was shocked and overwhelmed. We sat down and shared some details of our experience.

I headed to the back of the church and sat on what used to be the bleachers; they are no longer there. After a few minutes, a beautiful white-haired girl about sixteen sat next to me. She looked like an angel and had come from the front of the church. She put her soft white hair on my shoulder and simply sat there. I did not know what to think. It felt like the fellowship of heaven.

After a little bit, she raised her head and looked me in the eyes and said, "You really love, don't you?" I choked up, looked down at her wonderful little face and said, "Oh, yes."

She then said, "I know when I get to heaven and look into the Fathers eyes it will be like looking into your eyes."

I hung my head and wept softly. When I looked up, she was gone. After recovering some, I got up and staggered to the book-store. I knew the lady behind the counter and she turned around to look at me.

She stepped back and sighed, "I know when I get to heaven and look into the Fathers eyes it will be like looking into your eyes." I was undone.

Remember the two Korean girls? They came to me before the end of the service and asked if I could take them to the airport at six the next morning. I said yes and went to the motel where I was staying and checked out. I drove to their motel and checked in to make it easier for us.

I pulled up to airport departures to drop them off and said, "If for some reason you can't get on that flight, give me a call and I will come get you."

It was Saturday morning and I headed for the healing rooms at Bethel Church. After the healing rooms, I hit the road for home. After I bought gas and pulled out of the station to get on the freeway, there was an immediate check in my spirit.

I was not leave town. I argued with myself; seeing no reason to stay. Yet, I pulled around behind the service station and parked in the shade. For forty-five minutes I just watched the time go by. At eleven forty-five the phone rang. This soft little voice whispered, "Jack, can you still come and get us at the airport?"

Fifteen minutes later, I had these sweet, and a little sad, girls in the van. They told me they did not know why, but they could not get on the plane. After settling down, they asked if they could take me out for Thai food. At the time I did not like Thai food. So I said, "No, I will take you out for Chinese buffet — my treat."

As we pulled away from the Airport the girl in the back of the van said just out of the blue, "I saw a Winnie the Pooh poster in the airport. And the next time I see Winnie the Pooh, I will tell someone about Jesus." It was an off-hand comment and I rolled my eyes.

We found a perfect booth in the corner of the restaurant, loaded our buffet plates and finished the first round. The little girl that had mentioned her desire to share Jesus with Winnie the Pooh got up to refill her plate again. After she left, a waitress came by the table. She was Chinese and her name badge said "Winnie." The other girl and I looked at each other and we both began to cry. Soon the other girl came back with her plate filled with food. Winnie then told us, "People call me Winnie the Pooh."

Now we are doing the ugly cry and I was sliding under the table. The sweet girl put her plate down and went right to Winnie.

She grabbed her and with tears streaming down every face, told Winnie about Jesus and how much He loved her. It was the most wonderful time.